KNIT CELEBRITY Slouch
BEANIES *for the family*

You've seen them in magazines. You've watched them on TV. The rich and famous are wearing slouchy beanies wherever they go, and they look amazing! Now you can knit seven designs like those worn by movie stars, television personalities, and musicians. State your celebrity style in one of five high-fashion beanies for adults. If you know a toddler who loves to look adorable, make that tot a bright beanie with horizontal stripes! An older child will shine in the spotlight of your attention while wearing the two-in-one reversible beanie. All of these hats were designed by the talented Lisa Gentry to be great for casual days and every day —as well as for dodging the paparazzi!

Leisure Arts
Little Rock, Arkansas

Size: Small/Medium {Large/X-Large}
Fits Head Circumference: 21{23}"/53.5{58.5} cm

MATERIALS

Medium Weight Yarn (4) MEDIUM
[3$\frac{1}{2}$ ounces, 223 yards (100 grams, 205 meters) per skein]: 1 skein
16" (40.5 cm) Circular knitting needle, sizes 6 (4 mm) **and** 7 (4.5 mm) **or** sizes needed for gauge
Double-pointed knitting needles, size 7 (4.5 mm)
Marker
Yarn needle

GAUGE: With larger size needle, in Stockinette Stitch, 20 sts and 26 rows = 4" (10 cm)

Techniques used:
- K2 tog *(Fig. 4, page 31)*
- SSK *(Figs. 5a-c, page 31)*
- Slip 2 tog, K1, P2SSO *(Fig. 7, page 32)*

RIBBING

With smaller size needle, cast on 88{92} sts; place a marker to mark the beginning of the round *(see Markers, page 28)*.

Rnd 1 (Right side)**:** (K1, P1) around.

Repeat Rnd 1 until Ribbing measures approximately 1$\frac{3}{4}$" (4.5 cm) from cast on edge.

BODY

Change to larger size circular needle.

Rnd 1: Knit around increasing 24{34} sts evenly spaced *(see Increasing Evenly, page 31)*: 112{126} sts.

Work in Stockinette Stitch (knit every rnd) until piece measures approximately 8$\frac{1}{2}$" (21.5 cm) from cast on edge.

CAP SHAPING

Change to double-pointed needles when there are too few stitches to use a circular needle.

Rnd 1: ★ K1, SSK, K9, K2 tog; repeat from ★ around: 96{108} sts.

Rnds 2-4: Knit around.

Rnd 5: ★ K1, SSK, K7, K2 tog; repeat from ★ around: 80{90} sts.

Rnds 6-8: Knit around.

Rnd 9: ★ K1, SSK, K5, K2 tog; repeat from ★ around: 64{72} sts.

Rnds 10-12: Knit around.

Rnd 13: ★ K1, SSK, K3, K2 tog; repeat from ★ around: 48{54} sts.

Rnds 14-16: Knit around.

Rnd 17: ★ K1, SSK, K1, K2 tog; repeat from ★ around: 32{36} sts.

Rnds 18 and 19: Knit around. *Omit for Seamed hat or K3 18-19-20*

Rnd 20: ★ K1, slip 2 tog as if to **knit**, K1, P2SSO; repeat from ★ around: 16{18} sts.

Cut yarn leaving an 8" (20.5 cm) length for sewing. Thread yarn needle with end and weave through remaining sts; pull tightly to close and secure end.

Size: Small/Medium {Large/X-Large}
Fits Head Circumference: 21{23}"/53.5{58.5} cm

NATURALLY COMFORTABLE

MATERIALS

Medium Weight Yarn **MEDIUM 4**
[$3^1/_2$ ounces, 223 yards (100 grams, 205 meters) per skein]: 1 skein
16" (40.5 cm) Circular knitting needle, sizes 6 (4 mm) **and** 8 (5 mm) **or** sizes needed for gauge
Double-pointed knitting needles, size 8 (5 mm)
Marker
Yarn needle

GAUGE: With larger size needle, in Stockinette Stitch, 19 sts and 25 rows = 4" (10 cm)

Techniques used:
• P2 tog *(Fig. 6, page 32)*

RIBBING

With smaller size needle, cast on 100{104} sts; place a marker to mark the beginning of the round *(see Markers, page 28)*.

Rnd 1 (Right side)**:** (K2, P2) around.

Repeat Rnd 1 until Ribbing measures approximately $1^1/_2$" (4 cm) from cast on edge, increasing 0{6} sts *(see Zeros, page 29)* evenly spaced on last rnd *(see Increasing Evenly, page 31)*: 100{110} sts.

BODY

Change to larger size circular needle.

Rnds 1-8: (K3, P7) around.

Rnds 9 and 10: K4, P5, (K5, P5) around to last st, K1.

Rnds 11 and 12: K5, P3, (K7, P3) around to last 2 sts, K2.

Rnds 13-15: K6, P1, (K9, P1) around to last 3 sts, K3.

Rnds 16 and 17: K5, P3, (K7, P3) around to last 2 sts, K2.

Rnds 18 and 19: K4, P5, (K5, P5) around to last st, K1.

Rnd 20: (K3, P7) around.

Repeat Rnd 20 until piece measures approximately 8" (20.5 cm) from cast on edge.

CAP SHAPING
Change to double-pointed needles when there are too few stitches to use a circular needle.

Rnd 1: (K3, P2 tog, P5) around: 90{99} sts.

Rnd 2: (K3, P6) around.

Rnd 3: (K3, P2 tog, P4) around: 80{88} sts.

Rnd 4: (K3, P5) around.

Rnd 5: (K3, P2 tog, P3) around: 70{77} sts.

Rnd 6: (K3, P4) around.

Rnd 7: (K3, P2 tog, P2) around: 60{66} sts.

Rnd 8: (K3, P3) around.

Rnd 9: (K3, P2 tog, P1) around: 50{55} sts.

Rnd 10: (K3, P2) around.

Rnd 11: (K3, P2 tog) around: 40{44} sts.

Rnd 12: (K3, P1) around.

Cut yarn leaving an 8" (20.5 cm) length for sewing. Thread yarn needle with end and weave through remaining sts; pull tightly to close and secure end.

TRULY PURPLE

Size: Small/Medium {Large/X-Large}
Fits Head Circumference: 19{21}"/48.5{53.5} cm

Size Note: The sizing and Gauge are written for Small/Medium size with Large/X-Large size in braces { }. Follow the same instructions for **both** sizes. Final measurement is obtained by using a different needle size as recommended under Materials.

MATERIALS
Medium Weight Yarn [MEDIUM 4]
[3¹/₂ ounces, 223 yards (100 grams, 205 meters) per skein]: 1 skein
16" (40.5 cm) Circular knitting needle as indicated below **or** size needed for gauge
Small/Medium Size:
Sizes 6 (4 mm) **and** 8 (5 mm)
Large/X-Large Size:
Sizes 7 (4.5 mm) **and** 9 (5.5 mm)
Double-pointed knitting needles as indicated below:
Small/Medium Size:
Size 8 (5 mm)
Large/X-Large Size:
Size 9 (5.5 mm)
Cable needle
Marker
Yarn needle

GAUGE: With larger size needle, in Stockinette Stitch, 19{18} sts and 25{24} rows = 4" (10 cm)

Techniques used:
• M1 *(Figs. 3a & b, page 30)*
• K2 tog *(Fig. 4, page 31)*
• P2 tog *(Fig. 6, page 32)*

STITCH GUIDE
CABLE 2 FRONT
(abbreviated C2F) (uses 2 sts)
Slip next st onto cable needle and hold in **front** of work, K1 from left needle, K1 from cable needle.
CABLE 2 BACK
(abbreviated C2B) (uses 2 sts)
Slip next st onto cable needle and hold in **back** of work, K1 from left needle, K1 from cable needle.
CABLE 3 FRONT
(abbreviated C3F) (uses 3 sts)
Slip next 2 sts onto cable needle and hold in **front** of work, K1 from left needle, K2 from cable needle.

CABLE 3 BACK
(abbreviated C3B) (uses 3 sts)
Slip next st onto cable needle and hold in **back** of work, K2 from left needle, K1 from cable needle.

CABLE 4 FRONT
(abbreviated C4F) (uses 4 sts)
Slip next 2 sts onto cable needle and hold in **front** of work, K2 from left needle, K2 from cable needle.

CABLE 6 FRONT
(abbreviated C6F) (uses 6 sts)
Slip next 3 sts onto cable needle and hold in **front** of work, K3 from left needle, K3 from cable needle.

TWIST 3 FRONT
(abbreviated T3F) (uses 3 sts)
Slip next 2 sts onto cable needle and hold in **front** of work, P1 from left needle, K2 from cable needle.

TWIST 3 BACK
(abbreviated T3B) (uses 3 sts)
Slip next st onto cable needle and hold in **back** of work, K2 from left needle, P1 from cable needle.

RIBBING
With smaller size circular needle, cast on 99 sts; place a marker to mark the beginning of the round *(see Markers, page 28)*.

Rnds 1 and 2: ★ K4, P1, (K2, P1) twice; repeat from ★ around.

Rnd 3: ★ C4F, P1, (K2, P1) twice; repeat from ★ around.

Rnds 4-6: ★ K4, P1, (K2, P1) twice; repeat from ★ around.

Rnds 7-13: Repeat Rnds 3-6 once, then repeat Rnds 3-5 once **more**.

Rnd 14: ★ K1, P1, K2, M1, P1, (K2, P1) twice; repeat from ★ around: 108 sts.

BODY
Change to larger size circular needle.

Rnds 1-3: K1, P2, K2, P6, ★ K2, P2, K2, P6; repeat from ★ around to last st, K1.

Rnd 4: K5, P6, (K6, P6) around to last st, K1.

Rnd 5: ★ C4F, K1, P6, K1; repeat from ★ around.

Rnd 6: (K4, P8) around; remove marker, K1; place a marker to mark the beginning of the round.

Rnd 7: K3, P8, (K4, P8) around to last st, K1.

Rnd 8: ★ P2, C2F, P6, C2B; repeat from ★ around.

Rnd 9: ★ P2, K2, P6, K2; repeat from ★ around.

Rnd 10: ★ P2, T3F, P4, T3B; repeat from ★ around.

Rnd 11: P3, K2, (P4, K2) around to last st, P1.

Rnd 12: P3, T3F, P2, T3B, ★ P4, T3F, P2, T3B; repeat from ★ around to last st, P1.

Rnd 13: P4, K2, P2, K2, ★ P6, K2, P2, K2; repeat from ★ around to last 2 sts, P2.

Rnd 14: P4, C3F, C3B, ★ P6, C3F, C3B; repeat from ★ around to last 2 sts, P2.

Rnd 15: P4, K6, (P6, K6) around to last 2 sts, P2.

Rnds 16-18: P4, ★ K2, P2, K2, P6; repeat from ★ around to last 8 sts, (K2, P2) twice.

Rnd 19: P4, K1, C4F, K1, ★ P6, K1, C4F, K1; repeat from ★ around to last 2 sts, P2.

Rnd 20: P4, K6, (P6, K6) around to last 2 sts, P2.

Rnd 21: P5, K4, (P8, K4) around to last 3 sts, P3.

Rnd 22: P4, T3B, T3F, ★ P6, T3B, T3F; repeat from ★ around to last 2 sts, P2.

Rnd 23: P4, ★ K2, P2, K2, P6; repeat from ★ around to last 8 sts, (K2, P2) twice.

Rnd 24: P3, T3B, P2, T3F, ★ P4, T3B, P2, T3F; repeat from ★ around to last st, P1.

Rnd 25: P3, K2, (P4, K2) around to last st, P1.

Rnd 26: ★ P2, T3B, P4, T3F; repeat from ★ around.

Rnd 27: ★ P2, K2, P6, K2; repeat from ★ around; remove marker, K1; place a marker to mark the beginning of the round.

Rnd 28: ★ C3B, P6, C3F; repeat from ★ around.

Rnds 29-32: K3, P6, (K6, P6) around to last 3 sts, K3.

Rnd 33: K3, P6, (K6, P6) around to last 3 sts, K3; remove marker, K3; place a marker to mark the beginning of the round.

CAP SHAPING

Change to double-pointed needles when there are too few stitches to use a circular needle.

Rnd 34: ★ P2 tog, P2, P2 tog, C6F; repeat from ★ around: 90 sts.

Rnds 35-37: (P4, K6) around.

Rnd 38: ★ P2 tog, P2, K6; repeat from ★ around: 81 sts.

Rnd 39: (P3, K6) around.

Rnd 40: ★ P3, K1, K2 tog twice, K1; repeat from ★ around: 63 sts.

Rnd 41: (P3, C4F) around.

Rnds 42 and 43: (P3, K4) around.

Rnd 44: ★ P2 tog, P1, K4; repeat from ★ around: 54 sts.

Rnd 45: (P2, C4F) around.

Rnd 46: (P2, K4) around.

Cut yarn leaving an 8" (20.5 cm) length for sewing. Thread yarn needle with end and weave through remaining sts; pull tightly to close and secure end.

Size: Small/Medium {Large/X-Large}
Fits Head Circumference: 19{21}"/48.5{53.5} cm

Size Note: Instructions are written for Small/Medium size with Large/X-Large size in braces { }. Instructions will be easier to read if you circle all the numbers pertaining to your size. If only one number is given, it applies to both sizes.

MATERIALS

Medium Weight Yarn

[$3\frac{1}{2}$ ounces, 223 yards (100 grams, 205 meters) per skein]: 1 skein
16" (40.5 cm) Circular knitting needle, sizes 5 (3.75 mm) **and** 7 (4.5 mm) **or** sizes needed for gauge
Double-pointed knitting needles, size 7 (4.5 mm)
Cable needle
Marker
$1\frac{1}{8}$" (29 mm) Button - 1
Yarn needle
Sewing needle and thread

GAUGE: With larger size needle, in Stockinette Stitch, 20 sts and 26 rows = 4" (10 cm)

Techniques used:
- K2 tog *(Fig. 4, page 31)*
- P2 tog *(Fig. 6, page 32)*
- P3 tog *(Fig. 8, page 32)*

STITCH GUIDE
CABLE 4 FRONT
(abbreviated C4F) (uses 4 sts)
Slip next 2 sts onto cable needle and hold in **front** of work, K2 from left needle, K2 from cable needle.

RIBBING

With larger size circular needle, cast on 144{156} sts; place a marker to mark the beginning of the round *(see Markers, page 28)*.

Rnds 1-3: Knit around.

Change to smaller size circular needle.

Rnd 4: (P1, K2 tog) around: 96{104} sts.

Rnd 5: (P1, K1) around.

Repeat Rnd 5 until Ribbing measures approximately $2\frac{1}{2}$" (6.5 cm) from cast on edge, increasing 14{16} sts evenly spaced on last rnd *(see Increasing Evenly, page 31)*: 110{120} sts.

BODY

Change to larger size circular needle.

Rnds 1-4: ★ P7{8}, K4; repeat from ★ around.

Rnd 5: ★ P7{8}, C4F; repeat from ★ around.

Rnds 6-29: Repeat Rnds 1-5, 4 times; then repeat Rnds 1-4 once **more**.

CAP SHAPING

Change to double-pointed needles when there are too few stitches to use a circular needle.

Rnd 1: ★ P2 tog, P3{4}, P2 tog, C4F; repeat from ★ around: 90{100} sts.

Rnds 2-4: ★ P5{6}, K4; repeat from ★ around.

Rnd 5: ★ P2 tog, P1{2}, P2 tog, K4; repeat from ★ around: 70{80} sts.

Rnd 6: ★ P3{4}, C4F; repeat from ★ around.

Rnds 7 and 8: ★ P3{4}, K4; repeat from ★ around.

Size Small/Medium ONLY
Rnd 9: (P3 tog, K4) around: 50 sts.

Size Large/X-Large ONLY
Rnd 9: (P2 tog twice, K4) around: 60 sts.

Both Sizes
Rnd 10: ★ P1{2}, C4F; repeat from ★ around.

Rnd 11: ★ P1{2}, K4; repeat from ★ around.

Cut yarn leaving an 8" (20.5 cm) length for sewing. Thread yarn needle with end and weave through remaining sts; pull tightly to close and secure end.

CABLE BAND

With larger size circular needle, cast on 12 sts.

Row 1 (Right side)**:** Knit across.

Row 2: K3, P6, K3.

Rows 3-6: Repeat Rows 1 and 2 twice.

Row 7: K3, C6F, K3.

Row 8: K3, P6, K3.

Repeat Rows 1-8 for pattern until Cable Band measures approximately 19{21}"/48.5{53.5} cm from cast on edge, ending by working Row 8.

Buttonhole Row 1: K5, bind off next 2 sts, K4: 10 sts.

Buttonhole Row 2: K3, P2, **turn**; add on 2 sts *(Figs. 9a & b, page 32)*, **turn**; P2, K3: 12 sts.

Next Row: Knit across.

Last Row: K3, P6, K3.

Bind off all sts in **knit**.

FINISHING
Sew button to right side of cast on end of Cable Band.

Tack Cable Band to Hat.

Size: Small/Medium {Large/X-Large}
Fits Head Circumference: 19{21}"/48.5{53.5} cm

Size Note: Instructions are written for Small/Medium size with Large/X-Large size in braces { }. Instructions will be easier to read if you circle all the numbers pertaining to your size. If only one number is given, it applies to both sizes.

MATERIALS

Medium Weight Yarn
[5 ounces, 256 yards (140 grams, 234 meters) per skein]: 1 skein
16" (40.5 cm) Circular knitting needle, sizes 6 (4 mm) **and** 8 (5 mm) **or** sizes needed for gauge
Double-pointed knitting needles, size 8 (5 mm)
Marker
Yarn needle

GAUGE: With larger size needle, in Stockinette Stitch, 19 sts and 25 rows = 4" (10 cm); in Body pattern, 16 sts and 30 rows = 4" (10 cm)

Techniques used:
- K2 tog *(Fig. 4, page 31)*
- P2 tog *(Fig. 6, page 32)*

RIBBING
With smaller size needle, cast on 92{96} sts; place a marker to mark the beginning of the round *(see Markers, page 28)*.

Rnd 1 (Right side)**:** (K1, P1) around.

Repeat Rnd 1 until Ribbing measures approximately $1\frac{1}{2}$" (4 cm), increasing 19{25} sts evenly spaced on last rnd *(see Increasing Evenly, page 31)*: 111{121} sts.

BODY
Change to larger size circular needle.

Rnd 1: P1, (K1, P1) around.

Rnd 2: K1, (P1, K1) around.

Repeat Rnds 1 and 2 for pattern until piece measures approximately $5\frac{1}{2}$" (14 cm) from cast on edge, ending by working Rnd 2.

CAP SHAPING

Change to double-pointed needles when there are too few stitches to use a circular needle.

Rnd 1: ★ (P1, K1) 3 times, P2 tog, K2 tog; repeat from ★ around to last st, P1: 89{97} sts.

Rnd 2: K1, (P1, K1) around.

Rnd 3: P1, (K1, P1) around.

Rnd 4: K1, (P1, K1) around.

Size Small/Medium ONLY
Rnd 5: ★ P1, (K1, P1) 3 times, K2 tog, P2 tog, K1, (P1, K1) 3 times, P2 tog, K2 tog; repeat from ★ around to last st, P1: 73 sts.

Size Large/X-Large ONLY
Rnd 5: ★ (P1, K1) 4 times, P2 tog, K2 tog; repeat from ★ around to last st, P1: 81 sts.

Both Sizes
Rnd 6: K1, (P1, K1) around.

Rnd 7: P1, (K1, P1) around.

Rnd 8: K1, (P1, K1) around.

Rnd 9: ★ (P1, K1) twice, P2 tog, K2 tog; repeat from ★ around to last st, P1: 55{61} sts.

Rnd 10: K1, (P1, K1) around.

Rnd 11: P1, (K1, P1) around.

Rnd 12: K1, (P1, K1) around.

Rnd 13: P1, (K1, P1) around.

Size Small/Medium ONLY
Rnd 14: ★ K1, (P1, K1) twice, P2 tog, K2 tog, P1, (K1, P1) twice, K2 tog, P2 tog; repeat from ★ around to last st, K1: 43 sts.

Size Large/X-Large ONLY
Rnd 14: ★ (K1, P1) 3 times, K2 tog, P2 tog; repeat from ★ around to last st, K1: 49 sts.

Both Sizes
Rnd 15: P1, (K1, P1) around.

Rnd 16: K1, (P1, K1) around.

Size Small/Medium ONLY
Rnd 17: ★ P1, K1, P1, K2 tog, P2 tog, K1, P1, K1, P2 tog, K2 tog; repeat from ★ around to last st, P1: 31 sts.

Size Large/X-Large ONLY
Rnd 17: ★ (P1, K1)
twice, P2 tog, K2 tog;
repeat from ★ around to
last st, P1: 37 sts.

Both Sizes
Rnd 18: K1, (P1, K1)
around.

Rnd 19: P1, (K1, P1)
around.

Size Small/Medium ONLY
Rnd 20: ★ K1, P2 tog,
K2 tog, P1, K2 tog,
P2 tog; repeat from ★
around to last st, K1:
19 sts.

Size Large/X-Large ONLY
Rnd 20: ★ K1, P1,
K2 tog, P2 tog; repeat from
★ around to last st, K1: 25 sts.

Both Sizes
Rnd 21: P1, (K1, P1) around.

Cut yarn leaving an 8" (20.5 cm) length for sewing.
Thread yarn needle with end and weave through
remaining sts; pull tightly to close and secure end.

Size: Baby {Toddler}
Fits Head Circumference: 14{16}"/35.5{40.5} cm

MATERIALS

Medium Weight Yarn **[4]** MEDIUM

[$3^1/_2$ ounces, 170 yards (100 grams, 156 meters) per skein]:
MC - 1 skein
CC - 1 skein
16" (40.5 cm) Circular knitting needle, sizes 6 (4 mm) **and** 8 (5 mm) **or** sizes needed for gauge
Double-pointed knitting needles, size 8 (5 mm)
Marker
Yarn needle

GAUGE: With larger size needle, in Stockinette Stitch, 19 sts and 25 rows = 4" (10 cm)

Techniques used:
• K2 tog *(Fig. 4, page 31)*

STRIPE SEQUENCE

Rnds 1-3: CC.
Rnds 4-6: MC.
Rnds 7-12: Repeat Rnds 1-6.
Rnds 13 and 14: CC.
Repeat Rnds 1-6 for remainder of Hat.

RIBBING

With MC and smaller size needle, cast on 60{64} sts; place a marker to mark the beginning of the round *(see Markers, page 28)*.

Rnd 1 (Right side): (K2, P2) around.

Repeat Rnd 1 until Ribbing measures approximately $1^1/_4$" (3 cm), increasing 20{24} sts evenly spaced on last rnd *(see Increasing Evenly, page 31)*: 80{88} sts.

BODY

Change to larger size circular needle.

Working in Stripe Sequence, knit around until Hat measures approximately $4\{4^1/_2\}$"/10{11.5} cm from cast on edge.

CAP SHAPING

Change to double-pointed needles when there are too few stitches to use a circular needle.

Rnd 1: ★ K8{9}, K2 tog; repeat from ★ around: 72{80} sts.

Rnd 2: Knit around.

Rnd 3: ★ K7{8}, K2 tog; repeat from ★ around: 64{72} sts.

Rnd 4: Knit around.

Rnd 5: ★ K6{7}, K2 tog; repeat from ★ around: 56{64} sts.

Rnd 6: Knit around.

Rnd 7: ★ K5{6}, K2 tog; repeat from ★ around: 48{56} sts.

Rnd 8: Knit around.

Rnd 9: ★ K4{5}, K2 tog; repeat from ★ around: 40{48} sts.

Rnd 10: Knit around.

Rnd 11: ★ K3{4}, K2 tog; repeat from ★ around: 32{40} sts.

Rnd 12: Knit around.

Rnd 13: ★ K2{3}, K2 tog; repeat from ★ around: 24{32} sts.

Rnd 14: Knit around.

Cut yarn leaving an 8" (20.5 cm) length for sewing. Thread yarn needle with end and weave through remaining sts; pull tightly to close and secure end.

You get two hats in one with this cute reversible design!

Size: Toddler {Child}
Fits Head Circumference: 16{18}"/40.5{45.5} cm

Size Note: Instructions are written for Toddler size with Child size in braces { }. Instructions will be easier to read if you circle all the numbers pertaining to your size. If only one number is given, it applies to both sizes.

MATERIALS

Medium Weight Yarn
Version A (Blue):
[6 ounces, 315 yards (170 grams, 288 meters) per skein]: 1 skein
Version B (Variegated):
Shown on page 26
[3$\frac{1}{2}$ ounces, 223 yards (100 grams, 205 meters) per skein]: 1 skein
16" (40.5 cm) Circular knitting needle, sizes 6 (4 mm) **and** 8 (5 mm) **or** sizes needed for gauge
Double-pointed knitting needles, size 8 (5 mm)
Marker
Yarn needle

GAUGE: With larger size needle, in Stockinette Stitch, 19 sts and 25 rows = 4" (10 cm)

Techniques used:
• K2 tog *(Fig. 4, page 31)*

RIBBING

With smaller size needle, cast on 70{76} sts; place a marker to mark the beginning of the round *(see Markers, page 28)*.

Rnd 1: (K1, P1) around.

Repeat Rnd 1 until Ribbing measures approximately 1$\frac{1}{2}$" (4 cm), increasing 18{23} sts evenly spaced on last rnd *(see Increasing Evenly, page 31)*: 88{99} sts.

BODY

Change to larger size circular needle.

Rnd 1: ★ P1, K1, P1, K8; repeat from ★ around.

Rnd 2: K1, P1, (K 10, P1) around to last 9 sts, K9.

Repeat Rnds 1 and 2 until piece measures approximately 8{8$\frac{1}{2}$}"/20.5{21.5} cm from cast on edge, ending by working Rnd 2.

CAP SHAPING

Change to double-pointed needles when there are too few stitches to use a circular needle.

Rnd 1: ★ P1, K1, P1, K2 tog 4 times; repeat from ★ around: 56{63} sts.

Rnd 2: K1, P1, (K6, P1) around to last 5 sts, K5.

Rnd 3: ★ P1, K1, P1, K2 tog twice; repeat from ★ around: 40{45} sts.

Rnd 4: K1, P1, (K4, P1) around to last 3 sts, K3.

Rnd 5: ★ P1, K1, P1, K2 tog; repeat from ★ around: 32{36} sts.

Rnd 6: K1, P1, (K3, P1) around to last 2 sts, K2.

Cut yarn leaving an 8" (20.5 cm) length for sewing. Thread yarn needle with end and weave through remaining sts; pull tightly to close and secure end.

For Version A, turn inside out.

GENERAL INSTRUCTIONS

ABBREVIATIONS

C2B	Cable 2 Back	mm	millimeters
C3B	Cable 3 Back	P	purl
C2F	Cable 2 Front	P2SSO	pass 2 slipped stitches over
C3F	Cable 3 Front		
C4F	Cable 4 Front	Rnd(s)	Round(s)
C6F	Cable 6 Front	SSK	slip, slip, knit
CC	Contrasting Color	st(s)	stitch(es)
cm	centimeters	T3B	Twist 3 Back
K	knit	T3F	Twist 3 Front
M1	make one	tog	together
MC	Main Color		

★ — work instructions following ★ as many **more** times as indicated in addition to the first time. ( ) or [ ] — work enclosed instructions **as many** times as specified by the number immediately following **or** contains explanatory remarks. colon (:) — the number(s) given after a colon at the end of a row or round denote the number of stitches you should have on that row or round.

GAUGE

Exact gauge is **essential** for proper size. Before beginning your project, make a sample swatch in the yarn and needle specified in the individual instructions. After completing the swatch, measure it, counting your stitches and rows carefully. If your swatch is larger or smaller than specified, **make another, changing needle size to get the correct gauge**. Keep trying until you find the size needles that will give you the specified gauge.

HINTS

Good finishing techniques make a big difference in the quality of the piece. Always start a new ball at the beginning of a row or round, leaving ends long enough to weave in later. You can tie a loose knot close to the last stitch worked, but be sure to untie it before weaving in yarn ends. Thread a yarn needle with the yarn end. With **wrong** side facing, weave the needle through several stitches, then reverse the direction and weave it back through several stitches. When the ends are secure, clip them off close to work.

MARKERS

As a convenience to you, we have used markers to help distinguish the beginning of a round. Place a marker as instructed. You may use a purchased marker or tie a length of contrasting color yarn around the needle. When you reach a marker on each round, slip it from the left needle to the right needle; remove it when no longer needed.

KNIT TERMINOLOGY	
UNITED STATES	INTERNATIONAL
gauge =	tension
bind off =	cast off
yarn over (YO) =	yarn forward (yfwd) **or** yarn around needle (yrn)

KNITTING NEEDLES		
UNITED STATES	ENGLISH U.K.	METRIC (mm)
0	13	2
1	12	2.25
2	11	2.75
3	10	3.25
4	9	3.5
5	8	3.75
6	7	4
7	6	4.5
8	5	5
9	4	5.5
10	3	6
10½	2	6.5
11	1	8
13	00	9
15	000	10
17	---	12.75

Yarn Weight Symbol & Names	LACE 0	SUPER FINE 1	FINE 2	LIGHT 3	MEDIUM 4	BULKY 5	SUPER BULKY 6
Type of Yarns in Category	Fingering, size 10 crochet thread	Sock, Fingering, Baby	Sport, Baby	DK, Light Worsted	Worsted, Afghan, Aran	Chunky, Craft, Rug	Bulky, Roving
Knit Gauge Range* in Stockinette St to 4" (10 cm)	33-40** sts	27-32 sts	23-26 sts	21-24 sts	16-20 sts	12-15 sts	6-11 sts
Advised Needle Size Range	000-1	1 to 3	3 to 5	5 to 7	7 to 9	9 to 11	11 and larger

*GUIDELINES ONLY: The chart above reflects the most commonly used gauges and needle sizes for specific yarn categories.

** Lace weight yarns are usually knitted on larger needles to create lacy openwork patterns. Accordingly, a gauge range is difficult to determine. Always follow the gauge stated in your pattern.

ZEROS

Zeros are sometimes used so that all sizes can be combined. For example, knit 0{1-2} sts means the first size would do nothing, the second size would K1, and the largest size would K2.

KNITTING IN THE ROUND
USING CIRCULAR KNITTING NEEDLES

When you knit a tube, as for a hat, you are going to work around on the outside of the circle, with the right side of the knitting facing you. Using a circular knitting needle, cast on all stitches as instructed. Untwist and straighten the stitches on the needle to be sure that the cast on ridge lies on the inside of the needle and never rolls around the needle.

Hold the needle so that the ball of yarn is attached to the stitch closest to the **right** hand point. Place a marker on the right hand point to mark the beginning of the round.

To begin working in the round, knit the stitches on the left hand point **(Fig. 1)**. Continue working each round as instructed **without turning the work**; but for the first three rounds or so, check to be sure that the cast on edge has not twisted around the needle. If it has, it is impossible to untwist it. The only way to fix this is to rip it out and return to the cast on row.

Fig. 1

USING DOUBLE-POINTED KNITTING NEEDLES

When working a piece that is too small to use a circular knitting needle, double-pointed knitting needles are required. Divide the stitches into thirds and slip one-third of the stitches onto each of 3 double-pointed needles *(Fig. 2a)*, forming a triangle. Do **not** twist the cast on ridge. With the fourth needle, knit across the stitches on the first needle *(Fig. 2b)*. You will now have an empty needle with which to knit the stitches from the next needle. Work the first stitch of each needle firmly to prevent gaps. Continue working around without turning the work.

INCREASES
MAKE ONE
(abbreviated M1)

Insert the left needle under the horizontal strand between the stitches from the **front** *(Fig. 3a)*. Then knit into the **back** of the strand *(Fig. 3b)*.

Fig. 2a

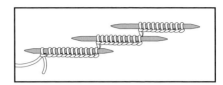

Fig. 2b

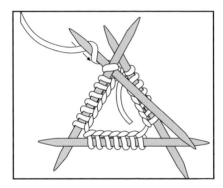

Fig. 3a

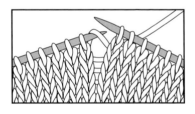

Fig. 3b

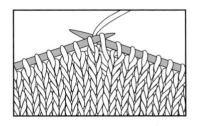

INCREASING EVENLY

Add one to the number of increases required and divide that number into the number of stitches on the needle. Subtract one from the result and the new number is the approximate number of stitches to be worked between each increase. Adjust the number as needed.

Fig. 4

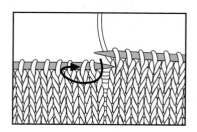

DECREASES
KNIT 2 TOGETHER
(abbreviated K2 tog)

Fig. 5a

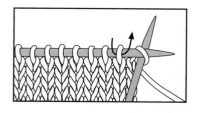

Insert the right needle into the **front** of the first two stitches on the left needle as if to **knit** *(Fig. 4)*, then **knit** them together as if they were one stitch.

Fig. 5b

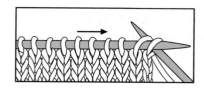

SLIP, SLIP, KNIT
(abbreviated SSK)

Fig. 5c

With the yarn in **back** of the work, separately slip two stitches as if to **knit** *(Fig. 5a)*. Insert the left needle into the **front** of both slipped stitches *(Fig. 5b)* then **knit** them together as if they were one stitch *(Fig. 5c)*.

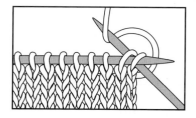

PURL 2 TOGETHER
(abbreviated P2 tog)
Insert the right needle into the **front** of the first two stitches on the left needle as if to **purl** *(Fig. 6)*, then **purl** them together as if they were one stitch.

Fig. 6

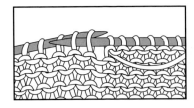

SLIP 2 TOGETHER, KNIT 1, PASS 2 SLIPPED STITCHES OVER (abbreviated slip 2 tog, K1, P2SSO)
Slip two stitches together as if to **knit**, then knit the next stitch. With the left needle, bring the two slipped stitches over the knit stitch and off the needle *(Fig. 7)*.

Fig. 7

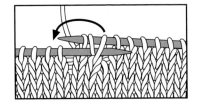

PURL 3 TOGETHER
(abbreviated P3 tog)
Insert the right needle into the **front** of the first three stitches on the left needle as if to **purl** *(Fig. 8)*, then **purl** them together as if they were one stitch.

Fig. 8

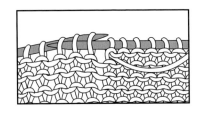

ADDING NEW STITCHES
Insert the right needle into the stitch as if to **knit**, yarn over and pull loop through *(Fig. 9a)*, insert the left needle into the loop just worked from **front** to **back** and slip the loop onto the left needle *(Fig. 9b)*. Repeat for the required number of stitches.

Fig. 9a

Fig. 9b

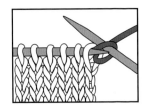

YARN INFORMATION

Each Beanie in this leaflet was made using Medium Weight Yarn. Any brand of Medium Weight Yarn may be used. It is best to refer to the yardage/meters when determining how many balls or skeins to purchase. Remember, to arrive at the finished size, it is the GAUGE/TENSION that is important, not the brand of yarn.

For your convenience, listed below are the specific yarns used to create our photography models.

Easy-Going
Patons® Classic Wool
#00227 Taupe

Casual Comfort
Red Heart® Soft Yarn
#4601 Off White

Naturally Comfortable
Patons® Classic Wool
#77010 Natural Marl

Fun Stripes
Lion Brand® Vanna's Choice® Baby
MC - #169 Sweet Pea
CC - #108 Bluebell

Truly Purple
Patons® Classic Wool
#00212 Royal Purple

Forward and Reverse
Version A:
Caron® Simply Soft® Brites
#9609 Berry Blue

Cabled Classic
Patons® Classic Wool
#00224 Grey Mix

Version B:
Patons® Classic Wool
#77014 Forest

Production Team: Technical Editors - Joan Beebe and Linda Daley; Contributing Editor - KJ Hay; Graphic Artists - Lora Puls, Becca Snider, Angela Stark, and Janie Wright; Photo Stylist - Angela Alexander; and Photographer - Jason Masters.

For digital downloads of Leisure Arts' best-selling designs, visit www.leisureartslibrary.com

ISBN- 13: 978-1-60900-093-6

EAN

50395

9 781609 000936

LEISURE ARTS
the art of everyday living
www.leisurearts.com

#75357 U.S. $3.95

0 28906 75357 8

MADE IN U.S.A.